# SATANIC SEAS
## DON'T DEFINE ME

# Ink Mistress

BookLeaf
Publishing
India | USA | UK

"What's in a name? That which we call a rose by any other name would smell as sweet."-Juliet, William Shakespeare, Romeo and Juliet.

"I am not bound to please thee with my answer."- William Shakespeare.

"I love you as certain dark things are to be loved, in secret, between the shadow and the soul."- Pablo Neruda

To my son, happiness, whose existence has been the greatest strength and inspiration.

# 1. changes

Every blow feels like thunder,
Striking the face of earth,
Radiating hollowness through zig zags of
gloaming.

Stones that held legacies
Disintegrate into the springs of firm
ground,
Camouflaging like finery of ash and dust.

If only changes were as peaceful as an
aftermath of a sunset,
Like blooming dahlias with a dash of
marigolds
And perfect strokes of hibiscus,
Taking me to a land of mild night falls,
Melodiously soothing the inner clusters,
Slow dancing to reflections of summer
songs.

## 2. Agitated pillows

Waking up within the wrong side of hell,
Time kept moving despite my body
suffocating without oxygen.
Injecting a plague of deceitful serenades
through doomed arteries,
A sledgehammer lay in a deep slumber
across a screaming heart.

Failing to protest against silhouette prints
on agitated pillows,
Gasping for air every two short breaths per
second,
Desperate to let out a scream from choking
dry backs of a sedated throat.

Could anyone hear the trembling panic,
Littered on flushed red cheeks turning
blue?
Could anyone bring my body back to
consciousness?

Alone within terrorized blankets of
counting fingers,
Curling those washed out toes into daring
fists,
Hoping a stiff bone would crack me open.

Finally, feeling fresh air gushing down
exhausted wind pipes,
I'm grateful for not being buried six feet
under,
Asleep forever on a graveyard mattress,
As if it's an open casket welcoming life
thirsty spirits
To jump into my empty vessel,
Rocking its way to an unfamiliar beginning
with the grim reaper,
Who's hiding behind empty corners of my
eyes.

Sadly awakening to deadly hallucinations
which left me frozen,
Never knowing when nightmares would die
and if life would set in.

## 3. Forsaken tales

Bound by the curved claws soaked in
wounded trust,
Ravenous wolves kept howling urban tales.
Scents from Eden's garden ran down their
spine,
As they captured repressed leaves left to
rust.
Mighty goodness fell into savored dust.
Eerie silence spilled into burned blood
drops.

And gypsy fairies emerged in dewdrops,
Striking darts of hope, for they knew no
trust,
Threw blood daggers across lawns of brick
dust.
Ancient hieroglyphics, paint these tales,
Crippling dreams that were left to rot in
rust.
Toes engraved with blood diamonds
through their spine.

Aphrodite slipped out of crooked spine.
Daisy chains failed to wipe away teal drops,
While war gods wrecked those Irish eyes to
rust.
Far beyond the grace left with bitter trust,
Losing tinted beauty in sapphire tales.
Every pain buried within ancient dust.

Away from mythological stardust,
Sprinting on edges of a fragile spine,
Searching for scripts of lost forgotten tales,
Creatures carried soft whispers in
sea-drops.
Emerald voyages found heart in trust.
In hopes of not letting their future rust.

Yet, what would an iron heart know of rust,
When all they've built were demolished to
dust
And nothing of love was in sight to trust?
Condemned fiercely by the devil's dark
spine,
They pledged along deep crimson river
drops,

Drowning in dungeons of forsaken tales.

Fooled from chronicles of demonic tales,
Infected nails hid beneath bolts of rust.
Roaring thunder exposed sinful raindrops,
No longer did they battle soils of dust.
Choked by cursed lines crawling between
their spine,
Finding consciousness within tainted trust.

Tales end with broken trails of pixie dust.
Rust from bars stand with their own wicked
spine.
Trust in plain shelters through their final
drops.

Form of poetry: Sestina

# 4. The sun of my life

Remember when we made paper planes in
carnivals of nursery rhymes,
When every meal was a game of 'catch me if
you can'?
I can still feel that blissful afternoon on a
scorching summer June,
When I first held you tightly, but gently in
my arms, promising to never fail you.
Often your cries lifted my amber skies,
wrapping them in hues of golden
aquamarine.
I still sense the embrace of your rosy pearl
divine,
When I sketched emerald lullabies from
every verse that fascinated you.
How I cradled you upon my lap,
Wishing your dreams would transcend
beyond this unforgiving earth.
Nobody needs to tell you how brave you
are;
Just like the deepest oceans, you have dived
through firestorms of emotions.

I still remember how those delicate little
hands carried finger-sized star fishes,
Placing them onto my palms.
A tiny gesture reminding me that I have
been carried within your honey thoughts,
As you swam among silver snappers and
slippery barnacles with your perfect fins
sloshing away waves, so melodiously
radiant.
Those innocent frowns stripped away every
dark stain that I ever had.
In a blink of an eye you have sprouted
branches stronger than I have ever known,
With dazzling stems that would prick any
killer bees around you.
An intelligent, beautiful force of nature that
mankind has ever known,
For you chime smarter and larger than your
humble mind perceives.
Those piercing copper eyes strike heavenly
arrows into every heart you've interacted.
Your contagious laughter fills up expanding
lungs with joy, as you banter with flawless
sarcasm.

How you love and wish to be loved, forms in
expressions through assembling comical
memes and rap songs,
To find homely creatures in your land of
humor,
Grateful for this marvelous gift as I cannot
imagine a life without your hands full of
delightful conversations.
Remember that you are the favorite part of
my everyday life,
And I shall protect you from the vermin of
this world's ungrateful pits.


Form of poetry: An Ode to my Son

# 5. Dreadful spines

For I was Present in my own absence,
Swamped cavernously in a wayward harm,
Sheltered within the wistful withdrawn
sense.

Suppressed silence echoed through the
gagged stress,
Transitioning nonsense from left to right.
Rob me from this aftermath of your mess
As I put on a historical fight.

Even Lilith loved from the spines of hate,
Savoring the tales of demonic thoughts
As cruel as her fists could confiscate.
I too shall rinse this nausea I caught.

Drenched by your delusional frozen rain,
Take note as they go down the dreadful
drain.

Form of Poetry: Sonnet

# 6. Unweary yearnings

Ever felt
The phenomenon
That floats among the
Limitless void?
Deep blue fluorites
Twinkle through these eyes;
Illusory skin
Speak in sins,
Invading the
Dark constellations
Hidden in my soul.
Tucked far along
Grey translucence
That coincide with
The radiance,
Emitting splendid
Teasings numbing
Unweary yearnings,
Stimulating pure
Jasmine waters
Into sweet seeds of
Of our galaxies

Glowing from a
Distance, as if our
Stars were about to
Explode into
Perfect implosions
In an exquisite
Ecstasy on
Strawberry velvet.

Form of Poetry: Anacreontic Verse

# 7. Satanic seas don't define me

In search of a sunken ship,
Preserved from a world of prying eyes,
She swims through echoing shells filled
with lies.
Her race is aquatic.
Her voice, a born true nomad,
Mythical traces of vitality,
Unyielding scales of divinity,
Ocean deep heart of invincibility,
Submerged in glaciers to silfra cracks.
Her amphibious scales breathe hope,
To swing from one melancholic wave to
another wave,
Floundering through trouts of tangs,
Like narrow rivers against colossal seas,
She heeds the midnight tales–dazed.
There roamed the whims and fantasies,
Snarky sand beds which lurked underneath
deep blue brine.
Shroud along ancient wicked streams,
unfold relief from sea serpents swirling
from blues to vicious yellows,

So naive, her heart, heard no other beat but
love!
In the spheres of greed and narcissism,
She remained an outcast,
Drenched in patch-coral caves, gravely
contrasted.

# 8. Unforgotten grave

Lined up against chained far flung doors,
You keep pushing through shields of
wordless fragments,
Hoping to hear tragic tales from this
concrete I walk on,
Like an eavesdropping choir outshining
grey clouds,
To dim my nostalgic moonlight,
Oblivious to heaving pounds of majestic
foreign haze,
Buried within too many metaphors turning
to flower dust,
Conquering skies swallowing seas in astral
serenity,
I found my voice through silence,
As Riotous blood seeped across hostile
valves,
Curses within calligraphic sketches, dark
enough to defy every forgotten and
unforgotten grave,
Persistently bled on endless surfaces from
razor quills,

Suffocated by gushing fog of betrayals,
Which shook every golden dust away from
shiny spectrums of my untethered skin,
Withered by pulling out skeletons from my
body, trying to orchestrate an exceptional
gospel for those starved ears,
For I molded curtain smiles, as I gathered
every autumn leaf and forbidden fruit
within infertile soils.
So let me bow out as you plead for my
submissiveness,
Let me bind these pages with complete
nothingness,
Let me trash the crowded rage filled with
your childishness,
As I follow the sun away from your
foolishness.

## 9. Forever, my angel

Sometimes words just don't come easy
When your heart is silenced,
As all that's left is a depiction of a manic
ambience,
Echoes of your laughter;
Oh Angelic hymns in my mind,
Like mellow Notes of a CorAnglais,
Engrossed in memories,
Breaking all bleeding arteries beneath my
chest,
I have Carved your name with Baleen plates
in every bottomless ocean,
For I know I will meet you again beneath a
painless sun,
Just you and I against all the odds.


Bradley: An Elegy for my Bestfriend

# 10. Edge of a dagger

Like an oracle with no heart,
She can be a soulless oppressor,
An insane damsel in distress,
Dwelling on gloomy strings as a cynical
mistress.
To love her would drive you to breathe on
the edge of a dagger,
As a hostage to heavily dripped tears behind
her throat,
Lashing out, swiping your sanity away, so
vigorously,
Drowning you deeper into diabolical seas,
Restrained for an eternity through her
raging pleas,
Though her pitch black soul craves for
affection,
Only to smother you in her tainted web of
obsession,
With Years full of stains constantly trying
to baptize the thieving deception,
For they froze her veins with malignant
manipulations,

And there she lay on the thorniest lawn,
Disinfecting the air which carried ghostly
whispers,
Breathing in blood boiling chemicals which
rot her vision,
Yet oceans played their part,
Reluctant to split open and draw a blissful
path,
Where love overpowered darkness from the
start,
Everything else slowly faded out,
As random forgiveness flew between two
beating hearts like tiny shooting stars.
Am I just hidden in your maze of charm?

# 11. Misinterpreted dreams

It seems like mutilated discomfort has
settled in permanently,
Putting us on a pedestal to ruthlessly
receive a weaponized experiment,
Ruffled and shuffled into a maddening
carousel with no escape from reality,
Sprinkling fantasies seeping out from
between our blinks,
While hunters and gatherers blindfold us
from what may or may not be,
As misinterpreted dreams turn into
illusionary fiction,
Fear lines up in the corner of our eyes
playing paranoid presumptions,
Drenching every hope down the drain,
Looking at every aid as the evil queen's
poisoned fruit,
For Lies were swaying to save us from what
they thought was irrational vandalism,
They may pour rains of sedation on our
raging confusion

To chain the demons from detonating into
the truth that hid behind our sense of
conscience,
Yet we have long caught the twists and
turns of society's emotional tools.
Would it take a divine and poetic soul to
stimulate alluring thoughts again?
Would an incomplete manuscript let us
compose our own destiny and fate?
Can the ignorant fools enshroud naive
hearts gloved helplessly with white stories?
Can they repaint the smoke stained walls
with golden glitter?
So just let us be one among the feathers of
an angelic truth.

# 12. melancholic aquarium

Time curves into a film of motionless
ripples,
As impossible as it may seem, cruelty can be
unbelievable.
The reality that feels exaggerated and
concocted with spoiling sea urchins,
So bitter and sour to comprehend,
Caving on her sacrificial showmanship,
Eyes that cast spells upon the sight of
roaring ovations,
Trying to dig through her doomed scales,
Clawing their way into her selfless mind,
The vampire squids paired along with
spider crabs,
Whispering words of deception to sway her
away from freedom.
She is no one's showcase.
Just like every wave that is strong and
powerful,
She too has risen from residues of bleached
corals;

A tiny slap of her tail could provoke the
loudest tides ever known.
A tribe of planktons circling her finger tips
like sparks emanating through her veins,
Blessing bliss upon her blue brines,
As life in an aquarium can be rather
melancholic.

## 13. her keeper

Beelzebub feasts
Upon my beloved fears.
Narcissistic demons,
Play wicked games
With empathic minds –
As she cries, I wipe my tears.

Diluted by his own promiscuousness,
Strolling in the shadows of her
vulnerabilities,
He absorbs her radiant spirit,
Like she is water to his infertile soil.
Yet she steers the pot,
As if it is a meal that will not rot,
An apricot that never decays,
But he lures her with grandiosity.
His kindness is an unkind energy,
She carries in brutal fluency.
For she knows of the abnormal, all too
normally.
He who demolishes her confidence,

Watches her petals wither under his
oppression.

Her blood covers his sins.
Hell bound, her hands open to the heavens.
For, she is surrounded by satanic seas,
Washing away ruined sandcastles of hope.
Unable to walk on water, her soul sinks like
the Titanic.
Waiting at the shore, she cries for a pilgrim
of love,
To set upon the path of pilgrimage to save
her.

## 14. That's love

Your Crystal clouds that simmer down my
poisoned pride, that's love.
Made this needle in a hay stack so
magnified, that's love

How can this soul swing any further
without your stone tide?
The fear fogged voice now orbits in your
throat worldwide, that's love.

Tracked my trail of footprints to scoop me
from the raven's guide,
To find simplest ways for two lost bones to
collide, that's love.

This blackened heart embraced by your
gaze, the perfect fireside.
Cracked ribs that knew pain now beats with
you side by side, that's love.

My possessions hold no weight, your home
is just me inside.

No gold nor silver would win my desires I
tried, that's love.


Form of Poetry: Ghazal

# 15. Orange blossoms and roses

Floating petals whisked
Perfumed wind from wet flowers
In Blooming orchards

Wild violets on
Melting mountains with strings of
Dew were sprouting life

As few spring fairies
Frisk around on fluffy clouds,
Sweet cherries rebirth

A lilac sunrise
Woke lady bugs on orange
Blossoms and roses

To stir valleys of murmur
And days of rainbows tremor


Form of Poetry: Haiku Sonnet

# 16. Quill of blood

I keep scribbling from my sleek bloody
quill,
Smothering the crooked scars in my art,
Strength in my limbs climb around thirsty
thrill.

Let these rhymes flow through my forsaken
will,
Cue the violins, as I speak this heart,
I keep scribbling from my sleek bloody
quill.

Knowing stings run along the pain I spill,
Even great storms would not keep us apart,
Strength in my limbs climb around thirsty
thrill.

Dare stop my pen from a poetic kill,
The shivering edge of a cold night's dart,
I keep scribbling from my sleek bloody
quill.

My pen draws empty blue prints to refill,
Songs of dead sea giving hints to restart,
Strength in my limbs climb around thirsty
thrill.

I am all metaphors, as torn out skill,
Medallion letters in silent depart,
I keep scribbling from my sleek bloody
quill,
Strength in my limbs climb around thirsty
thrill.


Form of Poetry: Villanelle

# 17. Poisoned chocolates

They question why I do what I do, do not
do.
What can a mind of realms do when what's
done is being done right in-front of my
face?
When everyone circles around calling me
crazy,
Forcing labels of different stages of insanity
upon me,
Pretending to know me from the rustic side
of a two faced coin,
And you call me a living madness.
How in this existing world would I feel at
home in a hardly noticeable zone,
Where everything and everyone is
everywhere and nowhere,
When uninvited confidantes keep knocking
on my door,
Holding bouquets of snakes,
Offering poisoned chocolates,
Trying to shove them down my suffocating
throat,

Attempting to convince me with their lies?
The insufferable simulated love that howls
in blood moonlight,
Fooling me with all their efforts, to drag me
down into depths of questioning my own
intelligence.
Yet you still misconceive me,
My matchbox tongue has an unpredictable
nature,
Which can ignite depending on the anguish
you have injected within me,
Rest your burdens under the palms of my
laughter,
For you will never be able to connect the
dots through my whirlwind of emotions,
I am tired of constantly looking over my
shoulders,
Wondering if those claws left a scar or a
bruise,
My turbulent past has enhanced these
knuckles,
Preparing for the first punch.
Resisting these deep irresistible train of
thoughts,

Fidgeting in the stillness with impulses of
premeditated paranoia,
Blanket of anxiety burns bridges faster than
I have created
From distraught efforts to avoid heartfelt
confrontations.
Intense rush of emotions characterized by
monsters,
The heart always hopes for warm affection,
But the mind is in conflict, pondering,
Should I drop my plate of blades embedded
deep within my bones,
Or am I an inconvenience expected to
entertain for your convenience.

# 18. Heretic aura, mom

She is the embodiment of an unforgotten
castle,
Castle where her waves of thunder are
stronger than any raging hurricane,
Hurricane that fears her hacksaw claws,
Claws digging deep into blood thirsty
wolves that prey upon her cubs,
Cubs that breathe under the spine of her
velvet roof,
Roof burning brighter than the devil's sun,
Sun shooting sinister colors framed in
sadistic gold,
Gold melting into silk from a single glance
through her walnut eyes,
Eyes that never slept over burning fireflies,
Fireflies shaking diabolical creatures back
to their dungeons of hell,
Hell in which they conjured evil schemes to
diminish her heretic aura,
Aura painting her blood in Persian
boldness,
Boldness primping her into elegance,

Elegance and radiance floating across
hushed aquamarine horizons,
Horizons swimming in the hopes of
painting orchids and shy lilies with lilac
butterflies,
Butterflies and winds swirl in her perfect
harmony,
Harmony which wiped away unfinished
apostrophes and question marks,
Marks tattooed across a mother's heartache,
Heartache that defines every maternal
struggle.


Form of Poetry: Loop Poem

# 19. Disappearing acts

If these wounds bleed scriptures for an
eternity,
Let them weep onto blank pages with
scarlet tears,
Scribbling painful nouns that carry verbs
for a  pronoun.
I build wings from sheets of verses,
Letting the wax melt into delicate layers of
my epidermis.
Some say beauty runs skin deep,
But all I have are haunted tales with
nightmares that weigh me down.
Maybe one day these calligraphic narratives
shall set me free,
Maybe one day I will close my eyes and
open them to flickering relief.
Over time when abiding, fading sun swiftly
leaves the sea,
Would there be a golden sense of release
setting by glacial mountains.
Am I to perpetually watch the stars be
pillars to heavy skies,

When my heart can be an open light azure,
Painted in orchid thistles and coral
paradigms?
When every walkway festooned with
sharpened bricks and splinters
Has repercussions of ugly restraints
blindfolding me?
Forcing me to feel like an irritable siren to a
deadly cyclone,
Like drizzling clouds to thunderous storms,
Fooling my mind with cowardly
disappearing acts,
Tiny twitches and lingering pauses.
A festering catastrophe waiting to unfold,
Pestering this mind into an undivided
entity of its own.

# 20. Mellifluous rhythms

Watching endless obscure sunsets
Paint shadows of misty yearnings,
Swirling to tempos choreographed with
mellifluous rhythms,
Sweet soft autumnal falls enhance my
dreams towards a kinder sphere,
As wild blue yonder synchronizes the very
nature of two overly smitten heartbeats.


Resting on untroubled cores of grass,
Whilst soaking in pebble droplets of spring
rain,
The tuscan sun has never beamed so
alluringly
To a fiesta of twilight that slowly fades,
As he gifts me innocent stems of tulips on
endless strings.
Stealing my heart, to magnetize it with his
soul,
Whilst arcadia gaze, witnessing aching
desires,
That scream no name but one called love,

He is the destiny assigned to mend these
pearly gates of my bones.

All I want is to bleed what I feel on his
untethered armor,
For I have found pieces of heaven in his
soothing lullabies,
Tuning like an angel sent from above,
Shielding me from the menace known as
life,
Awakening forsaken emotions through
humble beginnings,
Where twin flames rejuvenate with hope
and faith,
As if the thread of tones choose to diverge,
Whilst the dallying breeze of summer
forms alphabets of "forever".

## 21. make love to demons

So should I make love to flat lined demons
claiming to have empathy,
Or should I read between salty lies they
feed, like little micro monochrome needles,
Pricking intimate spaces in my head, while
they set camp on vulnerabilities,
Stomping like demolishing guardians
turning this psyche into permanent
insanity?
I can feel oxygen slowly condensing into
contaminated waters,
As my heart weeps with an uneven
thumping,
Disregarding any ability to harmonize these
valves.
How should I convince my mind that
everything is what it seems
Or as easy as words can be to rip off the
band aids blinding me,
While my body is the turbulence beating to
non-occurring disasters where
Terrifying tears keep shrieking in constant

terrors?
Asleep or awake, inhumane voices lurk
around as if I was a seven course buffet,
Slashing parts of me like a bloody rare
steak,
Feeding into my naivetés for dessert,
While I lay helplessly grasping for air.

## 22. strange and beautiful

Strange that you have majestically
crystallized your spine
With mighty wings and flaring burns,
Although I see you pretending to be strong,
Hiding beneath those scales they use as
battle shields,
Your scarlet illusory became a tale of
legendary power.
The flame you breathe out whispers firing
fears,
Yet your horns pierce right through my
nameless soul,
Latching your claws onto my diary of
nightmares,
Buried deep within a layer of poisonous
blood before you discovered it,
Should your silver blue jaws terrifically tear
the thin air to bits and pieces,
Or Should your opaque black eyes be
ignited by the fuel of my lungs and the
friction of my skin,
Without a shadow of doubt,

You paint the sun with your iridescent gold
dust,
Your skills beyond marvelous,
Adaptable to any given element,
Still my hands yearn to be the symbolic
border across your long grace.
And when hell lets loose,
You will find me on the edges of your legs,
Ushering you to another dimension of
where we truly belong.

## 23. splitting

Sometimes I fall in to pieces like acid rain
slapping a concrete jungle.
Every throbbing pipe inside of me aching
for just steady bliss,
In an era where masks are stir fried into the
skin of raw unrefined despair,
Nothing but this piece of blood
meat-beating it's way to disappointment in
fears,
Running out of ink to articulate these
cramps,
Canvas-ripped apart,
Drowning in an ocean of tears,
Fighting against every swell of the fuming
tides,
Gasping for the sun to calm the demons
that keep pouring down these drenched
lashes.
Time overpowers healing,
No street signs to guide you over barbed
glass.
Challenges through wall closing clusters,

And all I can see is the doorway to a clearer
dusk,
The salmon hues peeking through the
blinders, Tempting me to catch its glimpse
from my flesh!
A breeze that carries presence containing
all the rights without the wrongs!

## 24. you and i

Dreaming dreadful dreams,
In a room full of echoes.
Chilling sounds of whispering sobs,
tuned from a distant lullaby.
How terribly beautiful our words travel,
In the kind of music pain grooves too.
Engraved into my soul, the hues of you
Run out of rhymes, illustrating this love to
you.
Crimson tears scribble on my burnt diary
with charred pages.
Poetry is a fancy dress for pain.
Under the lines of the breeze,
We tuck away our secret melodies,
As my silenced scream ruffles from
emeralds to sapphires.
Your voice's stirred up emotions sleep
through everything before you,
As you are the chorus to all the love songs
we breed,
So come save me, take me away to a home of
just you and I.

## 25. the devil, I and the mystical creatures

The bedlam that drenched my soul in
silence?
Attempt to ruthlessly haul our patience,
Or thoughtless gambles on our ill psyche,
A blatant voice of doom to defy me.

Chronicles of the confined bird-revised,
The devil's portion had me mesmerized,
Planktons glowed every corner of my scars,
Scribbles of faith aligning the brim stars.

Mystical creatures of the briny deep,
The sharks, sting rays and crustaceans-they
weep,
And nature swayed to the same breeze as I,
That devious summer of cold july.

As I sighed, he discreetly seized my time,
Beautiful malediction as I rhyme.

## 26. Poetry overdose

Falling like screaming stars in jet black
distance,
We keep scribbling to express a little love,
Just a drizzle of our blooming existence.

Perfectly woven like an intertwined glove,
Harmlessly healing while caving in
shadows,
Oblivious to the sandy clouds above.

Spaced out cosmos of poetry overdose,
Breathing within forsaken dramatic strings,
Bled our somber thoughts to cold blooded
arrows.

Evolving poisoned petals of weeping
springs,
Never escaping green eyed evil monsters,
Puppeteers under thunderous storms of
kings.

Fighting slowly against ruthless imposters
And awakening to meaningless roosters.

Form of Poetry: Terza Rim

## 27. parched promises

April mornings are like a cup filled with
empty Wildfires,
Windswept silence trailed its way to choke
her for what felt like an eternity,
Parched promises dripped in heavy
dewdrops like threaded stars,
While silent misery swam through broken
love stories that hovered over the bed of
river Seine,
Yet echoing absurdity of inconvenient
conversations crawl onto wrinkled
midnight pillows,
And suffocates her once again as guilt sits
heavy like London air in 1850s,
Too cloudy to see any hues of hope.
Wept herself to cleanse her unholiness with
pellucid waters.
What have her sins drowned her into?
Was destiny such a cruel street with
barbaric eyes,
Or was her mind playing tricks once again?
Was she deliriously in a lucid dream once

again,
Searching for a never setting sun that
would paint her pain in churning colors,
Yearning to be an only embraced
masterpiece on the cracked walls of the
abandoned heart in ruin bars of Budapest?

## 28. the only beloved

Here I lay drowning in a sea of dandelions,
Once again lost without a plan,
As April showers took away my blissful
blooms,
Amber clouds washed away sweet scarlets
of spring.
Darts of bleak winter flung across emerald
lawns,
Whilst an indigo child awakened with
slumbering eyes from an ancient farewell.
Did you hear me weep under the willow
tree,
Or were wailings of my bleeding heart
insufficient,
to touch the dimmed crevasse of your
lethargic ice streams?
Mind you, my heart is not to be trifled with,
Though these yearnings pierce through
moonlit cruises,
My soul aches for your periwinkle
afterglows,
Like the aftermath of a coral rose sunset.

Let me be the only beloved in your khaki
closet.
Let me be the thread that weaves through
your ivory alabaster.
For I shall be a lost memory you will wish
to remember,
Just like that scribble in your memoirs,
when you found a diamond, rusting in the
sand.

# 29. forbidden freedom

If "we" are a sin,
Why is my heart bleeding for you?
Why is my soul screaming out your name?

Chained by the links of horrors
That hold me against you,
Towered high up above the ground,
Little did they know I'd crumble every bone
just for you.
I would not wish such adversity upon my
adversaries,
Such as the animosity which chastises our
hearts.

Every precious petal in my garden has
turned black,
Waiting for your lips to rejuvenate their
vibrant hues.
Why must love be cursed by society's
blindness,
Or has Cupid's ignorance plagued our
forbidden fate?

Maybe death is the only freedom for our devotion.

# 30. indigo nights

A scorching tale of sacred fire
Body tattooed with aching stars
Like night's sky with festering scars
Portions and spells trapped in barbed wire
An ocean of pitch black desire
Tangled in lost destinations
The stillness of these damnations
Mumblings of an indigo night
Triggered by an aggressive fright
So fight the portals through patience.

Form of poetry: The espinela is a
Spanish poetic form with two stanzas
and four end rhymes across 10 lines,
eight syllables per line.
Rhyme scheme is abba/accddc.
This form is also known as a decim.

# 31. when the reaper takes my soul

Sprouted seeds in pollinations of love,
Though spring blossoms twisted to shaggy
grey,
And dark butterflies they hovered above,
Shading tempting heat for the midnight
prey.

Think about all the lies that were secretly
fed.
Don't you dare cry for me when I am dead,
For there shall be nothing more left to weep
When the reaper takes my soul as I sleep.


Form of Poetry: rispetto (10 syllables
per line, 2 stanzas ,ababccdd)

# 32. I am yours

Sad
But true,
My heart no
Longer beams on
Its own, your husky
Mocha voice became an
Ornament through dim three-am
Midnight flares to fight fire in my
Bones with fire, and nothing else matters
When my Knees are driven to you like a
Blinded Moth to a dazzling flame, burning
Every sense in me to crave for your
Warm summery embrace. Take me
As I am and as I shall
Ever be. Oh master
Of puppets, let me
Be your starlight
In silence.
I am
Yours.

Form of Poetry: Double Etheree

Syllables go from one to ten and ten
to one, no rhyme scheme.

# 33. memories

When rooted promises shift through dust of
seasonal changes
From a kyanite summer breeze to blizzards
of painful longing,
Memories linger on, as nothing of value is
ever lost.

Form of Poetry: SIJO
It is a Korean verse form with three
lines. Each line consists of at least
14-16 syllables. With second line often
the longest.

# 34. imperfections

I am

Deeply lost in

Those imperfections that

Seem to be the reason you have

Ripened this tainted love: color me blind

Yet I see every flaw in you,

Severely torn apart

I sliced my wings

For you.


Form of Poetry: Rictameter (with a
syllable count of 2468108642).

# 35. OCEAN EYES

She will always remember that night at the
sun drenched beach;
A tiny getaway they found from ceaseless
cruising.
He had a way of making moonlight descend
from the twilight in her eyes,
Whilst softly swerving backwards along
the pristine shorelines.
Ocean listening to them sing their thalassic
hearts out,
Allowing a salty breeze to blow away the
ashes lying on forgotten gravel,
In Bermuda waters, where dried up hopes
lay buried at sea.
Hearts were lost under glowing dusts of
stars,
As turquoise waves met with sandy scars,
Oblivious to brown pelicans nesting afar
On sea grass beds contaminated in dead
coral reefs,
Disguising dreams within the ghastly hours
before dusk,

Unable to comprehend what lovers would
envision through trials and tribulations.
A mythical water nymph wearing a
prodigious seashell crown,
So unaware of the broken sharp translucent
stones
Piercing through her tail since birth.
A silent violence built up within her silvery
gills,
With tormented tears seeping into the
ground,
So breaking free was nothing but a mere
aspiration,
Until the palm trees sheltered her only
escape,
With the bravely armored mysterious soul,
Gathered in tangerine hints of an awakened
sunrise,
Floating on the grips of his suave arms.

# 36. FIGHT OR FLIGHT

She was lost in a mournful mist of an
unknown arena,
Drowning in an ocean of Beelzebub's
torment,
Like a haunting interrogation.
Filling the windpipes with
hyperventilations and blurred visions,
Fogging up her need to seek for the living.
Whilst constantly feeling like the sky is
closing down on an emotive shelf of
memories,
If only they saw the flashlight behind those
chestnut eyes,
Even sleep could not provide an ounce of
relief,
Though the devil's opera tethered onto the
consciousness,
Cultivating her thoughts into a house of
utter madness.
Pleading for recurring taunted nightmares
to vanish,
As she continuously run out of fingertips to

count,
when palpitating breaths full of fears
mounted.
There lay no humor in the perpetual
colorless layers of trauma,
As the thought of life and death pushed her
onto fight or flight instincts,
Stitching her open skin, to keep her from
unwelcomed flashbacks,
Yet her masked soul was swamped with fire
and ice,
Her mind sustained blood stained daisies,
As disguised bullets aiming at her sanity.
Sweeping away, rubbing on an empty
wishing lamp,
In hopes of seeing a beam of ray, wondering
if amnesia is the only remedy,
For her bones to stop aching from triggers
and tremors.

# 37. chrysalis

Like pollen stardust in an elysian universe,
Your hidden truth sprinkles across these
blazing flares.
If only they knew, every smile tells a story,
Tales we truly believe someone out there
will understand.
Although you camouflage the lustrous
ripples of secrets within fears,
I see you gasping for a gush of selenite air,
Trying to unleash yourself from fiendish
brass shackles,
Suffocating from the adversities of grieving
pilgrims.
Reminiscing tranquil realms that you once
roamed,
Along the gravels of emerald hilltops,
A naked chrysalis in need of saving, hiding
on empathetic treetops.
Too stubborn to acknowledge the
helplessness,
Whilst your nostalgic heart screams into
the pillows of your amour-less lungs,
You  keep walking alone in the dark,

expecting the moon to be blind,
But what would a broken soul foresee in a
world so unkind?
When your arms and knees walk on
autopilot,
Clearing the eye of storms in everyone's
blood stained sky,
You become oblivious to your own need for
eternal bliss,
As outsiders scornfully specify it as
forbidden fruit.
Here I stand at the peak of your shattered
dreams,
Let me hold your hand until you find
yourself again,
As you are lost in the shadows from
dripping wax fumes
That have eclipsed delicate, sensitive
sentiments.
Such are the healers that are shrouded in
collateral damage,
So let the pretty pastel rays beam into your
hibernating cocoon,
Until your wings blossom into a butterfly

touch,
Only meant for you and I.

# 38. Comfort in silence

Don't question my absence when I'm gone,
I find comfort in silence with repressed
memories playing on repeat.
Reminding me what it feels like from the
scent of secrets that they refused to fathom,
Though the mighty moon phases in and out
like deceptive mood swings,
Unable to comprehend the genesis of
treasured bruises,
As every scar obscures tragic tales untold,
What if they saw beneath this haunted skin
and fragile bones?
Would they understand where my darkness
transpired from,
Or would it be just another reason to frown
upon my dust filled mind?
What would the world know from those
moments of madness,
As they burned my existence like the
wilderness causes havoc on each other,
Labelling my needs as a succubus that floats
in Lilith's river,
Poaching on gullible souls in the slithering

summer?

Yet my legacy is engraved in their book of love within chapters of disaster.

## 39. maybe

Maybe I am just tired of listening to my
own demons playing tricks with my mind,
Exhausted from forcing out laughter
through my lungs.
Like I am carrying a swamp of nails
sticking into the back of my neck,
Twisting and turning, like a samba of pins
and needles down my spine.
Wormholes dancing tirelessly around my
chest,
Sucking the energy from any light that
dares to flash.
If only I knew the point of constant
endurance to not feel like a burden,
When everything I try to flourish seems to
dry out and die.
Looking forward seems to transcend into a
further distance,
So, I wander aimlessly, like a prolonged
pointless pilgrim.
Feels like my toes are chained to a gigantic
backbone of agony,

Ascending all paths more steeper than they
should be.
Maybe it's time to let go?
Or maybe it is just another psychotic
episode?
But all I know is, I am tired from holding
onto things that do not fit my fists.
When the current seems to stream against
my will,
When gravity keeps reminding me to hang
on,
Whilst certainty is laying under a
masquerade of fears and suppressed rage,
Tempted to turn away from
disappointment,
Persevering with patience and faith like a
stag's horn,
Slowly piercing through what strength is
left in me.
Maybe as I release my grip and let sands
flow in between my fingers,
Maybe then the weight would feel a little
more generous,
So I can finally rest my traumatized heart

within an eternal oblivion.
For the mirror knows I can't hide the
forbidden tears anymore.

# 40. splitting dusks and dawns

Somedays I write poetry,
Somedays poetry writes me,
Festering in gestures that makes me spin in
spirals,
Questioning the alignment of my existence.
Would I have been a better poet without the
turmoil,
Or would I have been just a deprived heart
with a soaring tumor?
Slowly plucking onto the wounds that
barely made their way to the surface,
You may count the amount of blood that
dripped onto the fields that danced along
the wind,
Nothing would weigh as heavy as the tears
I have collected on unslept nights.
Why bother build a home in such murky
darkness,
when the shadows are so unpredictable,
Unaware of the blades that run behind
featureless fog.
My soul yearns to be fed in the assurance of
your safety against the devil that lurks

under my toes.
Forgive me for I struggle to believe in the
sanctity of words,
As the weight of a hundred spears stand
firmly upon my spine,
Internally drowning me deeper within my
own fears,
Awaiting for the stars to play meteor
showers onto my demonic sky.
So purge away the story of redemption and
rebirth.
I am a loop of splitting dusks and dawns
trying to turn into a lost light,
Though a flammable breeze runs between
us.
Let there be no fire that may ignite another
catastrophic affliction.

# 41. fondant gates

The distance between us is nothing
compared to
how far I've fallen in love with you.
Despite the moon sleeping in your eyes,
I drift towards you like a galaxy of stars.
Craving your ivory fingers to unfurl my
ebony crest,
Flying me to thrilling northern lights, as I
grasp your fluttering wings onto my
heaving chest,
Enabling you to unravel and devour me,
under these artistically crumpled sheets,
Sprinkling sweetness across the mystifying
rivers of toffee loins that are ready to burst,
As you sensationally dive into these
restricted fondant gates,
To passionately feed beyond the luscious
linen,
Finding your way around enraptured
embodiment.
An enigmatic empress you've so effortlessly
tamed,
Conquering my walls whilst within a timid

pupa,
Confined inside the vulnerabilities of a
voiceless cocoon,
But waiting for your mystical vapors,
To unleash spring blooms in our souls,
Engraving "forever" on rose tinted glasses,
For summer steam has commenced calm
seas.
But these venereal spirits can run wild,
A vacant space that shall leave our eager
bodies to create reckless nights,
Feeling your claws ravishing their way onto
my back, deeper and faster,
Letting your hands explore like my
plesiosaurs guide,
As you set my body on fire with your
alluring tongue,
Whilst you grip onto my arches like a
momentous love ritual.
Like a scavenger hunting for hidden
passages,
Full of treasure and pleasure,
Sinfully scribbling about how tomorrow
shall be.

# 42. I sing my own stars

Some songs stay forever, some only for a
summer,
In need of a sun which is not like melted
butter on a toasty weather,
To heal my once broken heart with honey
coated pleasure,
Leisure that has only his silent name
engraved,
Though names have no meaning without an
immaterial soul,
Like an empty vessel traveling towards a
harbor with no sandy shores.
Whilst I found a lemonade heaven through
his tranquilizing voice,
That was just like him, swimming on a
daisy whim,
Caressing my urge to reach out to unseen
clouds that speak in stillness,
When magical moments danced below
micro oceanic stars,
So mysteriously silhouetting along the
turquoise tinted tides,
As the sweet heat tattooed my wet feet with

calligraphic ballads,
Unraveling tiny forgotten anecdotes that
laid just above the horizon,
Where the sun gently and slowly rests its
lips before it bids its last farewell,
Everything scrapes away like unknown
scatterings, meant to be blown away.
I sit by the beach, until my dolorous soul
peeled like rosy peach,
Letting scar marks to fall upon sharp
broken coral reefs,
Yet they failed to realize,
These bruises don't create my mantras, I
sing my own stars.

# ACKNOWLEDGEMENT

First and foremost, I would like to take a minute to express my deepest gratitude to the creator, God, for all those times, for giving inspiration through emptiness darkness, to find light through faith, nature and the miraculous universe.

Many thanks to my mom who always encouraged me to be a reader from a young age. Thank you for raising me into a world of words. I still remember the times when everything was blur and you gave me comfort through written pages from various authors. And that was my favorite memory of growing up. Thank you, mom. Because of you, I am not just a writer, but a reader too.

Thank you to my son. Your love and existence is the reason why I see light everyday. You are truly my only happiness and inspiration. I wouldn't want to change a thing about you, and you are more precious than any treasure could ever be. Together forever, I love you so much, my happiness.

To my twin sister, who has always been the reason behind my success, and not giving up. You have taught me to be strong and determined, even when the whole world tarnishes before my eyes! Thank you for helping me with everything and thank you for encouraging me to write this book, teaching me patience and tolerance. To take every step I can, to bloom into a better version of myself.

Thank you Dad, for teaching the importance of self respect and dignity, and showing what it is like to be in a man's world. You have always encouraged me to keep growing through learning, until the end of time. Your life lessons will be always treasured and it is a part of who I am today. Much love, always and forever.

To my cousin, Papi. No matter what, you always were there for me, made me laugh and kept me sane and safe. I appreciate you always and will always keep you close to my heart, my chocolate and make up partner! It's a blessing to have someone who can communicate on the some metaphorical level as I.

Thank you to my American Poodle, for always keeping the fire in me burning brighter and persuading to pursue writing.

Thank you to my beloved, my other half. Whom I can't live without. Twin flames destined to meet upon the stars across the sky. Your words flow through my veins and now you have become my home. You mean the world to me as we continue our journey in the cosmos together.

Thank you to poetic gardener, my partner in poetry, for guiding me to follow the light within me. Thank you for teaching me so much in so little time. You have made such a great impact in my world of writing through your mentoring and companionship. Thank you for being an important person in my life.

Thank you to my cousin A. You have always had my back. Together we phased and faced so much. I appreciate you so much.

Thank you Sara, for not leaving me alone in this world of madness, and showing me how beautiful it can be to be different. Together we grew through the storms of winter and summer as sisters from another misters! You will always be an important part of my life.

Thank you to @beginingofhope.ar for being one of the first supporters on Instagram. Your words of love has always inspired me.

Thank you to the writing community "poets_island". My beautiful islanders, your drive to learn and teach through kindness has been an inspiration during my writing journey on Instagram. I will forever be grateful for you all. Every islander means a lot to me. Along with "thoughtsallnight" my partner in the island community.

I won't forget the faithful ones. Although I haven't mentioned every name, you all mean a lot to me.


Thank you to all my readers and supporters and friends and family on Instagram writing community. I am not sure what I would do without you. Especially midnight coffee, Jules, for your kindness and support. Really means the world to me.

Thank you to the good and the bad and the ugly.

Thank you to the seasons that helped me channel through these emotions.

Thank you to the nostalgic sun and moon, for inspiring me.

Thank you mother nature. You have given a breathtaking circle of life.
Thank you to everyone who's hurt me just a little and even more.

Thank you to every kind hearted soul I've come across. You will all be a monument in my life.

Thank you to every single one of you who purchased my book and took the time to read. I appreciate you so much.